**Stage 4 More A
Songbirds Phonics**

Clare Kirtley

Teaching Notes

Contents

The Red Man and the Green Man

Pirates

Tails

Pen-Pals

My Cat

Tim's Bad Mood

Introduction

These books present highly decodable texts that children can read by sounding out and blending. They provide a reading context through which children can discover and understand that there is a code to reading. The explicit usefulness of phonics is emphasised in a variety of exciting reading books, all by popular, award winning children's author, Julia Donaldson.

The focus phonics are listed on the cover of each book. By introducing these and the skills of sounding out and blending prior to reading, the children will be equipped with the necessary knowledge to confidently and successfully read unfamiliar words in the books. The books consolidate letter-sound knowledge and practise the skills of sounding out and blending, reinforcing decoding as a reading strategy that children can use to become fluent, independent and capable readers. These notes describe activities to learn the focus phonics prior, during and after group or independent reading. The amount of time spent introducing the phonics prior to reading will of course depend on the ability of the children.

The inclusion of words that do not use the focus phonics being introduced or studied previously has been kept to a minimum while keeping the texts meaningful. Such words, often high frequency words, can be introduced and compared with the decodable words before studying the texts. The children can be encouraged to read such words in the text using several reading strategies such as sounding out, rereading to check it makes sense, context and sight vocabulary. Therefore such words are listed as 'Context' words.

These books provide the ideal resource for children to decode, understand and reflect on what has been written, responding to the varied ideas, themes and events and thus engaging in reading for pleasure. They fully support a synthetic approach to teaching reading and follow the introduction of grapheme-phoneme correspondences outlined in *Playing with Sounds*.

Glossary

Phoneme – a sound in a word (e.g. *cat, shop, sky, light* and *rain* all have three phonemes or three separate sounds)

Grapheme – a letter or sequence of letters that represents a phoneme (e.g in *rain* each of the three phonemes is represented by a grapheme *r – ai – n*; in *light* each of the three phonemes is represented by a grapheme, namely *l – igh – t*.

Context words – words which do not use the focus phonics but which are needed for the story.

The Red Man and the Green Man

Focus phonics	Skills, concepts and knowledge covered by the Teaching Notes	
Revision of phonics from Stages 1+, 2, 3, 4 ee as in *three* (made by *ee*, *ea*, *e*, *y*) ie as in *tie* (made by *ie*, *i-e*, *igh*, *i*) oe as in *toe* (made by *oa*, *ow o-e*, *o*) ai as in *train* (made by *ai*, *ay a-e*, *a*)	***Skills*** – Blend sounds together to read words; Segment words into their individual sounds for writing; Hear and differentiate between short and long vowel sounds in words ***Concepts*** – A sound in a word can be represented by one letter or by more than one letter; There can be more than one way to represent a sound; The same spelling pattern can represent more than one sound ***Knowledge*** – Focus phonics	**Example phonic words** Again snail train day holiday say stays make waves a green keeps see sees beach sea seaside tea he we happy cries inside seaside lights right I I'm road home don't go going know knows

Context words
the live people they of these says one goes have two to some roll are into all here do what

Letters and sounds Phase 5	PNS Literacy Framework Y1
A sound in a word can be represented by one letter or by more than one letter; There can be more than one way to represent a sound; The same spelling pattern can represent more than one sound	**W** 5.2, 5.3, 5.4, 5.5, 5.6, 5.7 6.1, 6.2, 6.3, 6.4 **C** 7.1 12.1

Pirates

Focus phonics	Skills, concepts and knowledge covered by the Teaching Notes	
Revision of phonics from Stages 1+, 2, 3, 4 ee as in *three* (made by *ee*, *ea*, *e*, *y*) ie as in *tie* (made by *i-e*, *igh y*, *i*) oe as in *toe* (made by *oa*, *ow o-e*, *o*) ai as in *train* (made by *ai*, *ay*, *a-e*, *a*)	***Skills*** – Blend sounds together to read words; Segment words into their individual sounds for writing; Hear and differentiate between short and long vowel sounds in words ***Concepts*** – A sound in a word can be represented by one letter or by more than one letter; There can be more than one way to represent a sound; The same spelling pattern can represent more than one sound ***Knowledge*** – Focus phonics	**Example phonic words** sail wait away play Jade wakes wave a asleep between deep feel feels need sees sleep eat begins he me hungry fifty fire like mine quite time while write fight fighting lights my shy I I'm I've I'll boats load hole know don't go gold no opens so

Context words
pirate for comes to the of have they we've you want

Letters and sounds Phase 5	PNS Literacy Framework Y1
A sound in a word can be represented by one letter or by more than one letter; There can be more than one way to represent a sound; The same spelling pattern can represent more than one sound	 5.2, 5.3, 5.4, 5.5, 5.6, 5.7 6.1, 6.2, 6.3, 6.4 7.1 11.1, 11.2 12.1, 12.2

Focus phonics	Skills, concepts and knowledge covered by the Teaching Notes	Example phonic words / Context words	Letters and sounds	PNS Literacy Framework
Revision of phonics from Stages 1+, 2, 3, 4 ee as in three (made by ee, ea, e, y) ie as in tie (made by ie, i-e, y, i) oe as in toe (made by oa, ow, o) ai as in train (made by ai, ay, a-e, a)	**Skills** – Blend sounds together to read words; Segment words into their individual sounds for writing; Hear and differentiate between short and long vowel sounds in words **Concepts** – A sound in a word can be represented by one letter or by more than one letter; There can be more than one way to represent a sound; The same spelling pattern can represent more than one sound **Knowledge** – Focus phonics	**Example phonic words** whale bobtail tail tails away play stingray chase shapes snake waves a amazing scaly sees three whee eat eats leap peacock be he she happy pony puppy scaly stumpy lion flies like likes sizes white crocodile by I'll goat burrow show go going opens pony so **Context words** of have all to do her wants you the	Phase 5 A sound in a word can be represented by one letter or by more than one letter; There can be more than one way to represent a sound; The same spelling pattern can represent more than one sound	**Y1** **W** 5.2, 5.3, 5.4, 5.5, 5.6, 5.7 6.1, 6.2, 6.3, 6.4 **G** 7.1 12.1

Focus phonics	Skills, concepts and knowledge covered by the Teaching Notes	Example phonic words / Context words	Letters and sounds	PNS Literacy Framework
Revision of phonics from Stages 1+, 2, 3, 4 ee as in three (made by ee, ea, e, y) ie as in tie (made by i-e, igh, y, i) oe as in toe (made by oa, o-e, o) ai as in train (made by ai, ay, a-e, a)	**Skills** – Blend sounds together to read words; Segment words into their individual sounds for writing; Hear and differentiate between short and long vowel sounds in words **Concepts** – A sound in a word can be represented by one letter or by more than one letter; There can be more than one way to represent a sound; The same spelling pattern can represent more than one sound **Knowledge** – Focus phonics	**Example phonic words** afraid again wait Friday May play playing stay game made make name plane safely a meet see feast read reading be me she we granny safely sorry twenty very crocodile like nine time midnight my shy Friday hi I I'm quiet Joan Joan's home jokes broken crocodile don't go no told **Context words** your school the you are have one do to come of love sneeze was today can't goes	Phase 5 A sound in a word can be represented by one letter or by more than one letter; There can be more than one way to represent a sound; The same spelling pattern can represent more than one sound	**Y1** **W** 5.2, 5.3, 5.4, 5.5, 5.6, 5.7 6.1, 6.2, 6.3, 6.4 **G** 7.1 12.1

My Cat

Focus phonics	Skills, concepts and knowledge covered by the Teaching Notes	Example phonic words		
Revision of phonics from Stages 1+, 2, 3, 4 ee as in *three* (made by ee, ea, e, y) ie as in *tie* (made by i-e, igh, y, i) oe as in *toe* (made by ow, o-e, o) ai as in *train* (made by ai, ay, a-e, a)	**Skills** – Blend sounds together to read words; Segment words into their individual sounds for writing; Hear and differentiate between short and long vowel sounds in words **Concepts** – A sound in a word can be represented by one letter or by more than one letter; There can be more than one way to represent a sound; The same spelling pattern can represent more than one sound **Knowledge** – Focus phonics	again tail say stay whale a keeps feeling sea me silly suddenly time write bright my try find I I'll I'm I've know window nose rose cold going poem so won't		
		Context words to head about out of the you can't		
		Letters and sounds Phase 5 A sound in a word can be represented by one letter or by more than one letter; There can be more than one way to represent a sound; The same spelling pattern can represent more than one sound		**PNS Literacy Framework** Y1 **W** 5.2, 5.3, 5.4, 5.5, 5.6, 5.7 6.1, 6.2, 6.3, 6.4 **C** 7.1 12.1

Tim's Bad Mood

Focus phonics	Skills, concepts and knowledge covered by the Teaching Notes	Example phonic words		
Revision of phonics from Stages 1+, 2, 3, 4 oo as in *moon* (made by oo)	**Skills** – Blend sounds together to read words; Segment words into their individual sounds for writing; Hear and differentiate between short and long vowel sounds in words **Concepts** – A sound in a word can be represented by one letter or by more than one letter; There can be more than one way to represent a sound; The same spelling pattern can represent more than one sound **Knowledge** – Focus phonics	mood bedroom food spoon too stool boots pool		
		Context words the are said		
		Letters and sounds Phase 5 A sound in a word can be represented by one letter or by more than one letter; There can be more than one way to represent a sound; The same spelling pattern can represent more than one sound		**PNS Literacy Framework** Y1 **W** 5.2, 5.3, 5.4, 5.5, 5.6, 5.7 6.1, 6.2, 6.3, 6.4 **C** 7.1 12.1

The Red Man and the Green Man

> **Focus phonics**
>
> Revision of phonics from Stages 1+, 2, 3, 4
> *ee* as in *three* (made by *ee ea e y*)
> *ie* as in *tie* (made by *ie i-e igh i*)
> *oe* as in *toe* (made by *oa ow o-e o*)
> *ai* as in *train* (made by *ai ay a-e a*)

> **C** = Language comprehension
> **W** = Word recognition
> *AF* = QCA Assessment focus

Revisit, review and teach

W *Quick sounds*
Use a letter fan to revise previously learnt letter patterns for the focus long vowel sounds. Ask the children to say the sound made by each letter pattern as you hold it up.

W *Robot talk*
Place objects (or pictures of objects) that are written with the focus long vowel letter patterns in a bag (e.g. *train, clay, game, sheep, seat teddy, tie, knight, kite, coat, crow, rope*). Use a toy to name the things in the bag in a special robotic way. Tell the children the toy says all the sounds in words separately and they have to blend the sounds together to tell you what the toy is saying. Ask the children to take turns to be the toy.

W Write each of the words for *Robot talk*. Ask the children to highlight the letter pattern in each word which makes the long vowel sound. Ask the children to say the sound of each letter pattern as you point to it, then blend the letters together to read each word.

Group or guided reading

Before reading

Ⓦ Explain that it is important when blending together the sounds in a word, to check to see if it sounds like a real word as some words are less regular. Remind the children of the context words (see the inside back cover of the book) by writing them on a whiteboard. Read these words and point out the letters that make the usual sound in each word (e.g. the *l* in *live*).

Strategy check

Ⓦ Ask the children to tell you the long vowel sound made by each letter pattern in the box on the back cover of the book. Tell the children that some of the words in this book use these letter patterns so they should look out for them, remembering to sound out and blend words they do not recognise.

Independent reading

Encourage each of the children to read the whole book at his or her own pace, pointing at the words, sounding out and blending words they do not recognise. Listen in to each child reading and provide praise and support.

● Praise the children for sounding out and blending sounds to read words they do not recognise, and for recognising familiar words.

Assessment Observe the children to check that they can:

■ *(AF1)* confidently give the sound for all the focus letter patterns

■ *(AF1)* successfully blend the sounds of the words *holiday* and *seaside* together by blending the sounds in each syllable together first.

Emphasise and model these skills for any child who needs help.

Returning to the text

Ask the children to

Ⓒ *(Clarifying)* Tell you if the red man and the green man liked their holiday. Find some evidence in the book to support their view. (No, because no one stops when the red man tells them and no one goes when the green man tells them.)

Ⓦ Find some words in the text with a long *ai* vowel sound (*they, day, holiday, train, stays, make, waves, snail, a, say, again*). Read all the words except the frequent word *they*, by sounding out and blending.

(W) Shut the book, segment the words *day, train, say, make,* and *snail* into their separate sounds and write the words on a whiteboard. Underline the letter pattern in each word which makes the long vowel sound.

(W) Tell you whether the *ai* letter pattern occurs in the middle or end of the words. Repeat for *ay.*

Assessment Observe the children to check that they can:

- *(AF2)* follow the meaning of the text, going beyond the literal and locating evidence
- *(AF1)* identify, sound out, blend and read words containing the long vowel sound *ai*
- *(AF1)* segment words into their separate sounds, remembering the letter patterns which represent those sounds
- *(AF1)* analyse the letter patterns used to write the long vowel sound *ai.*

Model the appropriate responses for children who need help. Follow this up with further practice using the Stage 4 activities and talking stories on the Songbirds CD-ROM.

Where next?

Further phonic practice

(W) *Word sort*
Make five columns labelled with a different spelling pattern for the long vowel sound *ie* (*ie, igh, i, i-e, y*). Find words from the text containing the long vowel sound *ie.* Segment each word into its separate sounds and write it in the appropriate column. Tell the children to look out for new words to add.

Extension phonic work

(W) *Speed read*
You will need a list of words using the focus phonics for each child (e.g. *brain, take, say, tray, snake, we, sleep, sheet, speak, funny, jolly, chain, clean, flame, been, me, play*) and a timer. Start the timer and ask the children to sound out and read as many of the words as they can before the time runs out.

Pirates

Focus phonics

Revision of phonics from Stages 1+, 2, 3, 4
ee as in *three* (made by *ee ea e y*)
ie as in *tie* (made by *i-e igh y i*)
oe as in *toe* (made by *oa ow o-e o*)
ai as in *train* (made by *ai ay a-e a*)

C = Language comprehension
W = Word recognition
AF = QCA Assessment focus

Revisit, review and teach

W *Quick sounds*

Use magnetic letters to revise previously learnt letter patterns for the focus long vowel sounds. Ask the children to say the sound made by each letter pattern as you place it on a board.

W Practise blending sounds. Use the magnetic letters to write words with the focus long vowel sounds on the board (e.g. *my, cry, light, sprain, shine, low, going, stay, floating, late, scream, tried, lion, street*). Ask the children to draw a sound button under each letter pattern and underline the letter pattern in each word that makes the long vowel sound. Ask all the children to sound out the letter patterns as you point to them and blend them together again to read each word.

Group or guided reading

Before reading

W Explain that it is important when blending together the sounds in a word, to check to see if it sounds like a real word as some words are less regular. Remind the children of the context words (see the inside back cover of the book) by writing them on a whiteboard. Read these words and point out the letters that make the usual sound in each word (e.g. the *c* in *comes*). This will help the children to remember these words.

Strategy check

Ask the children to tell you the long vowel sound made by each letter pattern in the box on the back cover of the book. Tell the children that some of the words in this book use these letter patterns so they should look out for them as they read, remembering to sound out and blend words they do not recognise.

Independent reading

(W) Encourage each of the children to read the whole book at his or her own pace, pointing at the words, sounding out and blending words they do not recognise. Listen in to each child reading and provide lots of praise and support if necessary.

● Praise the children for sounding out and blending sounds to read words they do not recognise.

● Praise the children for recognising familiar words.

Assessment Observe the children to check that they can:

■ *(AF1)* confidently give the sound for all the focus letter patterns

■ *(AF1)* successfully blend the sounds of the words *hungry* and *fighting* together by blending the sounds in each syllable together first.

Emphasise and model these skills for any child who needs help.

Returning to the text

Ask the children to

(C) *(Clarifying)* Tell you if the pirates fight and why. Find some evidence in the book to support their view. (They do not fight because they like each other.)

(W) Find some words in the text with a long *ie* vowel sound (*pirate, I, while, my, mine, fight, I'm, I've, time, lights, fire, fighting, quite, like, shy, write, I'll*). Read all the words, by sounding out and blending.

(W) Shut the book, segment the words *my, mine, quite, fighting* and *shy* into their separate sounds and write the words on a whiteboard. Underline the letter pattern in each word that makes the long vowel sound.

(W) Tell you whether the letter pattern *y* usually occurs in the middle or end of words (end).

Assessment Observe the children to check that they can:

- *(AF2)* follow the meaning of the text, going beyond the literal and locating evidence
- *(AF1)* identify, sound out, blend and read words containing the long vowel sound *ie*
- *(AF1)* segment words into their separate sounds, remembering the letter patterns which represent those sounds
- *(AF1)* analyse the letter patterns used to write the long vowel sound *ie*.

Model the appropriate responses for children who need help. Follow this up with further practice using the Stage 4 activities and talking stories on the Songbirds CD-ROM.

Where next?

Further phonic practice

Ⓦ *Word sort*
Make five columns, four columns labelled with a different spelling pattern for the long vowel sound *oe* (*oa, ow, o, o-e*) and one labelled 'unusual'. Find words from the text containing the long vowel sound *oe*. Segment each word into its separate sounds and write it in the appropriate column. Tell the children to look out for new words to add to the sets.

Extension phonic work

Ⓒ *(Imagining)* Ask the children to work in pairs to discuss the characters and to make up a character profile of each pirate.

Ⓦ Ask the children to use their profiles to write letters to one another and to read each other's letters, by sounding out then blending words which they do not recognise. They can then write a reply.

Tails

Focus phonics

Revision of phonics from Stages 1+, 2, 3, 4
ee as in *three* (made by *ee ea e y*)
ie as in *tie* (made by *ie i-e y i*)
oe as in *toe* (made by *ow o oa*)
ai as in *train* (made by *ai ay a-e a*)

C = Language comprehension

W = Word recognition

AF = QCA Assessment focus

Revisit, review and teach

W *Quick sounds*
Use a letter fan to revise previously learnt letter patterns for the focus long vowel sounds. Ask the children to say the sound made by each letter pattern as you hold it up.

W *Spot the long vowel sound.*
Tell the children that you are going to say some words that contain long vowel sounds. Ask the children to spot which of the words have the same long vowel sound in them. Say *snail, shake, stone*. Write the words the children spot on a whiteboard (*snail, shake*). Repeat with *spray, no, slow; bright, brain, bike; lay, road, joke;* and *nine, feet, stream*.

W Look at the list of words. Ask the children to draw a sound button under each letter pattern and underline the letter pattern in each word that makes the long vowel sound. Ask all the children to sound out the letter patterns as you point to them and blend them together again to read each word.

Group or guided reading

Before reading

W Explain that it is important when blending together the sounds in a word, to check to see if it sounds like a real word as some words are less regular.

Remind the children of the context words (see the inside back cover of the book) by writing them on a whiteboard. Read these words and point out the letters that make the usual sound in each word (e.g. the *w* in *wants*). This will help the children to remember these words.

Strategy check

Ask the children to tell you the long vowel sound made by each letter pattern in the box on the back cover of the book. Tell the children that some of the words in this book use these letter patterns so they should look out for them as they read, remembering to sound out and blend words they do not recognise.

Independent reading

W Encourage each of the children to read the whole book at his or her own pace, pointing at the words, sounding out and blending words they do not recognise. Listen in to each child reading and provide lots of praise and support if necessary.

● Praise the children for sounding out and blending sounds to read words they do not recognise.

● Praise the children for recognising familiar words.

Assessment Observe the children to check that they can:

■ *(AF1)* confidently give the sound for all the focus letter patterns

■ *(AF1)* successfully blend the sounds of the words *stingray* and *peacock* together by blending the sounds in each syllable together first.

Emphasise and model these skills for any child who needs help.

Returning to the text

Ask the children to

C *(Clarifying)* Tell you some of the animals in the text which have tails (*cat, dog, kitten, puppy, rabbit, squirrel, fox, fish, stingray, snake, pony, peacock*).

W Write the animal words on a whiteboard. Segment the words into separate sounds, write the sounds down then blend them together to read what they have written. Look in the book to check.

W Find some words in the text with a long *oe* vowel sound (*go, burrow, going, so, pony, opens, show*). Read all the words by sounding out and blending.

(W) Shut the book, segment the words *show* and *burrow* into their separate sounds and write the words on a whiteboard. Underline the letter pattern in each word that makes the long vowel sound.

(W) Tell you whether the *ow* letter pattern usually occurs in the middle or end of words (end).

Assessment Observe the children to check that they can:

- *(AF1)* follow the meaning of the text recalling significant parts
- *(AF1)* segment words into their separate sounds, remembering the letter patterns which represent those sounds
- *(AF1)* identify, sound out, blend and read words containing the long vowel sound *oe*
- *(AF1)* analyse the *ow* letter pattern.

Model the appropriate responses for children who need help. Follow this up with further practice using the Stage 4 activities and talking stories on the Songbirds CD-ROM.

Where next?

Further phonic practice

(W) *Word sort*
Make five columns, four columns labelled with a different spelling pattern for the long vowel sound *ee* (*ee, ea, e, y*) and one labelled 'unusual'. Find words from the text containing the long vowel sound *ee*. Segment each word into its separate sounds and write it in the appropriate column. Tell the children to look out for new words to add to the sets.

Extension phonic work

(W) Ask the children to think of other words which rhyme with *tail*. Discuss how the long vowel sound is written in these rhyming words. Encourage the children to use a dictionary to check. (Some words are spelled with *ai* like *ail, pail, mail, snail, nail, fail, trail*, and some with *a-e* like *sale, pale, male, whale*. There are also exceptions such as *veil*.)

Pen-Pals

Focus phonics

Revision of phonics from Stages 1+, 2, 3, 4
ee as in *three* (made by *ee ea e y*)
ie as in *tie* (made by *i-e igh y i*)
oe as in *toe* (made by *oa o-e o*)
ai as in *train* (made by *ai ay a-e a*)

C = Language comprehension
W = Word recognition
AF = QCA Assessment focus

Revisit, review and teach

W *Quick sounds*
Use magnetic letters to revise previously learnt letter patterns for the focus long vowel sounds. Ask the children to say the sound made by each letter pattern as you place it on a board.

W Practise blending sounds. Use the magnetic letters to write words with the focus long vowel sounds on the board (e.g. *creep, cloak, tight, cream, window, open, sly, frame, slime, soap, playing, cried, she, hole, holly, drain*). Ask the children to draw a sound button under each letter pattern and underline the letter pattern in each word that makes the long vowel sound. Ask all the children to sound out the letter patterns as you point to them and blend them together again to read each word.

Group or guided reading

Before reading

W Explain that it is important when blending together the sounds in a word, to check to see if it sounds like a real word as some words are less regular. Remind the children of the context words (see the inside back cover of the book) by writing them on a whiteboard. Read these words and point out the letters that make the usual sound in each word (e.g. the *h* in *have*). This will help the children to remember these words.

Strategy check

Ask the children to tell you the long vowel sound made by each letter pattern in the box on the back cover of the book. Tell the children that some of the words in this book use these letter patterns so they should look out for them as they read, remembering to sound out and blend words they do not recognise.

Independent reading

Ⓦ Encourage each of the children to read the whole book at his or her own pace, pointing at the words, sounding out and blending words they do not recognise. Listen in to each child reading and provide lots of praise and support if necessary.

● Praise the children for sounding out and blending sounds to read words they do not recognise.

● Praise the children for recognising familiar words.

Assessment Observe the children to check that they can:

▪ (AF1) confidently give the sound for all the focus letter patterns

▪ (AF1) successfully blend the sounds of the words *reading* and *midnight* together by blending the sounds in each syllable together first.

Emphasise and model these skills for any child who needs help.

Returning to the text

Ask the children to

Ⓒ (Clarifying) Tell you if Joan and Megan enjoyed their time together. Find some evidence in the book to support their view. (Yes, because Megan writes in her diary *I am missing Joan* and Joan writes to Megan *I had such a fab time with you*.)

Ⓦ Find some words in the text with a long *ee* vowel sound (*twenty, be, we, sneeze, read, reading, meet, me, sorry, see, she, very, Granny, feast, safely*). Read all the words, by sounding out and blending.

Ⓦ Shut the book, segment the words *twenty, reading, sorry, see, she* and *Granny* into their separate sounds and write the words on a whiteboard. Underline the letter pattern in each word that makes the long vowel sound.

Ⓦ Tell you whether the letter pattern *y* usually occurs in the middle or end of words (end).

Assessment Observe the children to check that they can:

- *(AF2)* follow the meaning of the text, going beyond the literal and locating evidence
- *(AF1)* identify, sound out, blend and read words containing the long vowel sound *ee*
- *(AF1)* segment words into their separate sounds , remembering the letter patterns which represent those sounds
- *(AF1)* analyse the letter patterns used to write the long vowel sound *ee*.

  Model the appropriate responses for children who need help. Follow this up with further practice using the Stage 4 activities and talking stories on the Songbirds CD-ROM.

Where next?

Further phonic practice

W *Word sort*

Make five columns, four columns labelled with a different spelling pattern for the long vowel sound *ai* (*ai, ay, a, a-e*) and one labelled 'unusual'. Find words from the text containing the long vowel sound *ai*. Segment each word into its separate sounds and write it in the appropriate column. Tell the children to look out for new words to add to the sets.

Extension phonic work

W Give cards to the children, showing the previously learnt letter patterns, *ai, ay, ee, ea, y, igh, ie, oa, ow, o, g, p, f, l, n, t*. Call out a word and ask all the children to segment the word into its separate sounds. Then ask all the children who are holding a card showing a letter pattern needed to write the sounds in that word, to come out to the front to make the word. Ask all the children to blend the sounds together as you point to each letter pattern to read the new word to see if it is correct. Words to say are *play, low, pie, glow, lay, pain, tea, fly, leap, float, goal, light, lie, go, paint, no, feel, flow, tie, feet, faint, neat, night, goat.*

My Cat

Focus phonics
Revision of phonics from Stages 1+, 2, 3, 4 *ee* as in *three* (made by *ee ea e y*) *ie* as in *tie* (made by *i-e igh y i*) *oe* as in *toe* (made by *ow o-e o*) *ai* as in *train* (made by *ai ay a-e a*)

C = Language comprehension

W = Word recognition

AF = QCA Assessment focus

Revisit, review and teach

W *Quick sounds*

Use a letter fan to revise previously learnt letter patterns for the focus long vowel sounds. Ask the children to say the sound made by each letter pattern as you hold it up.

W Practise segmenting and blending sounds. Write words with long vowel sounds on cards and place them in a bag (e.g. *coat, sweet, fly, playing, so, knee, cried, lake, night, strain, eating, hungry, slime, stone, growing*). Ask the children to work in pairs with a letter fan. Ask one child to pick one of the cards from the bag and read the word without showing it to the rest of the children. Ask the other children to work together to segment the word into all its sounds and then use the letter fan to write the word. Look at the word on the card to check if it is written correctly. Ask all the children to read the word by sounding out and blending.

Group or guided reading

Before reading

W Explain that it is important when blending together the sounds in a word, to check to see if it sounds like a real word as some words are less regular. Remind the children of the context words (see the inside back cover of the book) by writing them on a whiteboard. Read these words and point out the letters that make the usual sound in each word (e.g. the *h* in *head*).

Strategy check

Ask the children to tell you the long vowel sound made by each letter pattern in the box on the back cover of the book.

Independent reading

(W) Encourage each of the children to read the whole book at his or her own pace, pointing at the words, sounding out and blending words they do not recognise. Listen in to each child reading and provide lots of praise and support if necessary.

● Praise the children for sounding out and blending sounds to read words they do not recognise.

● Praise the children for recognising familiar words.

Assessment Observe the children to check that they can:

■ *(AF1)* confidently give the sound for all the focus letter patterns

■ *(AF1)* successfully blend the sounds of the words *humpback*, *window* and *feeling* together by blending the sounds in each syllable together first.

Emphasise and model these skills for any child who needs help.

Returning to the text

Ask the children to

(C) *(Clarifying)* Tell you some of the things the girl unsuccessfully tries to write a poem about (*mum and dad, sea and sand, a bright red rose, humpback whale*).

(W) Write the things on a whiteboard. Segment the words into separate sounds, write the sounds down then blend them together to read the words. Look in the book to check.

(W) Find the words in the text which rhyme with *dad, sand, rose* and *whale* (*pad, hand, nose, tail*). Read all the words by sounding out and blending.

(W) Shut the book, segment the words *tail* and *nose* into their separate sounds and write the words on a whiteboard. Underline the letter pattern that makes the long vowel sound in these words.

(W) Write some more words which rhyme with *nose* (e.g. *those, hose, blows, crows*).

Assessment Observe the children to check that they can:

- *(AF1)* follow the meaning of the text recalling significant parts
- *(AF1)* segment words into their separate sounds, remembering the letter patterns which represent those sounds
- *(AF1)* identify, sound out, blend and read words which rhyme
- *(AF1)* generate words which rhyme and segment them into their separate sounds to write.

Model the appropriate responses for children who need help. Follow this up with further practice using the Stage 4 activities and talking stories on the Songbirds CD-ROM.

Where next?

Further phonic practice

(W) Ask the children to work in pairs and give each pair a whiteboard and pen. Tell the children pairs of rhyming words (e.g. *he/she, holly/jolly, coat/boat, say/tray, hope/rope, feet/sheet, light/might, coal/foal, me/he, try/sky*). Ask the children to work together to segment the words into separate sounds, write the sounds down on the whiteboard, then blend them together to read what they have written.

(W) Ask the children to write other pairs of rhyming words which have a long vowel sound and then to underline the letter pattern that makes the long vowel sound in each word.

Extension phonic work

(W) *Speed read*
You will need a list of words using the focus phonics for each child (e.g. *play, tie, team, kite, strain, happy, cry, window, meet, flake, sigh, toad, midnight, beside, broke, sunny, plate, flies, stealing*) and a timer. Start the timer and ask the children to sound out and read as many of the words as they can before the time runs out. Ask them to count the number of words correctly read as their score. Repeat several times so that the children can better their own previous score. Send the lists home for homework.

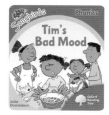

Tim's Bad Mood

Focus phonics	
Revision of phonics from Stages 1+, 2, 3, 4 **oo** *as in* moon *(made by* oo)	mood bedroom food spoon too stool boots pool

C = Language comprehension

W = Word recognition

AF = QCA Assessment focus

Revisit, review and teach

W *Quick sounds*

Use magnetic letters to revise previously learnt letter patterns for the focus long vowel sounds. Ask the children to say the sound made by each letter pattern as you place it on a board.

W Practise blending sounds. Use the magnetic letters to write words with the focus long vowel sounds on the board (e.g. *feed, time, rain, spray, cheat, only, show, silly, rope, bowl, sty, fright, begin, croak, plane*). Include words with the letter pattern *oo* as in *moon* and remind the children of the long vowel sound this letter pattern can make (e.g. *spoon, soon, broom, cool, hoot*). Ask the children to draw a sound button under each letter pattern and underline the letter pattern in each word that makes the long vowel sound. Ask all the children to sound out the letter patterns as you point to them and blend them together again to read each word.

Group or guided reading

Before reading

W Explain that it is important when blending together the sounds in a word, to check to see if it sounds like a real word as some words are less regular.

Remind the children of the context words (see the inside back cover of the book) by writing them on a whiteboard. Read these words and point out the letters that make the usual sound in each word (e.g. the *s* in *said*).

Strategy check

Ask the children to tell you the long vowel sound made by each letter pattern in the box on the back cover of the book.

Independent reading

(W) Encourage each of the children to read the whole book at his or her own pace, pointing at the words, sounding out and blending words they do not recognise. Listen in to each child reading and provide lots of praise and support if necessary.

● Praise the children for sounding out and blending sounds to read words they do not recognise.

● Praise the children for recognising familiar words.

Assessment Observe the children to check that they can:

■ *(AF1)* confidently give the sound for all the focus letter patterns

■ *(AF1)* successfully blend the sounds of the words *rainbow* and *lumpy* together by blending the sounds in each syllable together first.

Emphasise and model these skills for any child who needs help.

Returning to the text

Ask the children to

(C) *(Summarising)* Tell you if Tim is happy with his clothes. Find some evidence in the book to support their view (No, *his hat is too red, his coat is too green, his boots are too tight, his socks are too smelly, his top is too old, his trunks are too spotty*).

(W) Write some of his complaints on a whiteboard. Segment the words into separate sounds, write the sounds down then blend them together to read what they have written. Look in the book to check.

(W) Underline the letter pattern that makes the *oo* sound in *boots*. Find other words in the text which contain the letter pattern *oo* as in *boots* (*mood, bedroom, food, spoon, too, stool, pool*). Read the words by sounding out and blending.

Observe the children to check that they can:

- *(AF2)* follow the meaning of the text, going beyond the literal and locating evidence
- *(AF1)* segment words into their separate sounds , remembering the letter patterns which represent those sounds
- *(AF1)* identify, sound out, blend and read words containing the long vowel sound *oo* as in *boots*.

Model the appropriate responses for children who need help. Follow this up with further practice using the Stage 4 activities and talking stories on the Songbirds CD-ROM.

Where next?

Further phonic practice

Ⓦ Ask the children to read the last word in each sentence by sounding out and blending, then decide which of these words rhyme (*food/mood, high/ shy, green/mean, tight/bright, old/cold, lumpy/grumpy*). Give the children a whiteboard and pen. Ask the children to write the rhyming words on the whiteboard and underline the letter pattern that makes the long vowel sound in each word.

Ⓦ Ask the children to write other pairs of rhyming words which have a long vowel sound and then to underline the letter pattern that makes the long vowel sound in each word.

Extension phonic work

Ⓦ Give cards to the children, showing the previously learnt letter patterns, *ai, ay, ee, ea, y , igh, ie, oa, ow, o, oo, n, t, r, s, w, b*. Call out a word and ask all the children to segment the word into its separate sounds. Then ask all the children who are holding a card showing a letter pattern needed to write the sounds in that word, to come out to the front to make the word. Ask all the children to blend the sounds together as you point to each letter pattern to read the new word to see if it is correct. Words to say are *tray, soon, try, sway, row, no, tree, so, by, train, boat, stray, root, say, tie, way, sigh, see, right, seat, bow, neat, boot, brain, bee.*

Oxford Reading Tree resources at this level

There is a range of material available at a similar level to these stories which can be used for consolidation or extension.

Stage 4

Teacher support
For developing phonological awareness
- Rhyme and Analogy First Story Rhymes
- Rhyme and Analogy First Story Rhymes Tapes
- Alphabet Frieze
- Tabletop Alphabet Mats,
- Alphabet Photocopy Masters
- Card Games

Further reading
- ORT Floppy's Phonics
- ORT First Phonics
- Snapdragons Stories
- Glow-worms Poetry
- Fireflies and More Fireflies Non-Fiction

Electronic
- First Phonics Talking Stories and activities
- First Story Rhymes
- Rhyme and Analogy Activity Software
- Talking Stories
- Clip Art
- Storytapes
- Floppy and Friends CD-ROM
- eSongbirds CD-ROM
- ORT Online www.OxfordReadingTree.com

OXFORD
UNIVERSITY PRESS

Great Clarendon Street, Oxford OX2 6DP

Oxford University Press is a department of the University of Oxford.
It furthers the University's objective of excellence in research,
scholarship, and education by publishing worldwide in

Oxford New York

Auckland Cape Town Dar es Salaam Hong Kong Karachi
Kuala Lumpur Madrid Melbourne Mexico City Nairobi
New Delhi Shanghai Taipei Toronto

With offices in

Argentina Austria Brazil Chile Czech Republic France Greece
Guatemala Hungary Italy Japan Poland Portugal Singapore
South Korea Switzerland Thailand Turkey Ukraine Vietnam

Oxford is a registered trade mark of Oxford University Press
in the UK and in certain other countries

© Oxford University Press 2007

The moral rights of the author have been asserted

Database right Oxford University Press (maker)

First published 2007

British Library Cataloguing in Publication Data

Data available

Cover illustration by Andy Parker

ISBN: 978-0-19-911754-3

10

Paper used in the production of this book is a natural, recyclable product made
from wood grown in sustainable forests. The manufacturing process conforms
to the environmental regulations of the country of origin.

Printed in China by Imago